The Ocean Carries Me

Poems

*For Marianne!
an amazing woman!*

♡ *Gerda*

GERDA WALZ-MICHAELS

GENTLE ACTIONS

To the reader:

I invite you to read the silence expressed in the blank pages of this book. When we allow ourselves to be suspended in space and time an opening may occur.

FOR

DAVID

OLIVER

VANESSA

REBEKAH

SUSANNAH

DAISY

ELENA

AND

BUBBI

CONTENTS

FOREWORD

These poems were written in the time frame of about twelve years, from 1999 to 2011. The poems are spun in loose chronological order from 1942, the year of my birth, to 2011, the year of my youngest brother's death.

The collection starts with "A Prayer," which lies at the center of my search for clarity in my life. It continues with "Anonyma," the story of a young woman who experienced the end of World War II, living alone in Berlin. These two poems give direction to my work as being both very personal and going beyond personal, reaching out to understand that period in history.

I spent the first forty years of my life in Germany. At the end of this time, while visiting London, a shift of continents took place. After that I lived in America, regularly traveling between the two continents. I started to encounter feelings from the past and the present times in all different forms and intensities and wrote them down in poems or essays, thus opening up a change of perception. Different bodies of water - the Atlantic, the North and Baltic Seas, lakes and rivers - played a crucial role.

Coming to the last of my poems before the Epilogue I can honestly express a "Thank you" for my life's many blessings. It became more transparent and clear to me. I had lived with the burden of Germany's Nazi past, subconsciously and consciously, all my life. This is at least how I felt. Being silenced from childhood on, I continued to be silent many more years until I confronted myself finally with this silence, which showed up in my body and soul through all sorts and degrees of pain. Slowly, a transformation began to take place, accompanied by improved health, strength, acceptance and gratitude. Writing the poems led me to more forgiveness, both given and received. It changed my life.

LOST

A PRAYER

Born 1942
in Germany.

How can I be other than sad.

At the end in 1945
six million Jews dead.

Only you know and can help.

ANONYMA

Just three months more
and the brutal war would be over.
She could not have known.

She lived only to save her life.
Rape and abuse belonged to her daily chores
like getting bread and water, depending

solely on the Russian soldiers
who came conquering the city.

She worked herself up
to majors and higher officers

to be protected from the too many
others of lower rank, and

she got through, survived
and lived a quiet life after that.

Her diary, written so well,
was made into a book

published many years later, but
she preferred to stay anonymous.

MY MOTHER

My mother died when I was nine.
I was the last of her five children.
She had me in her late thirties.
My third child was born late as well,
in my mid-forties.

When I was very young, she got cancer.
My father and my grandmother knew,
but nobody told her or us. There was
an unbearable silence.
It was the time of World War II.

The last years of her life
became alive to me only recently,
by discovering photos, and letters
which she wrote to my sister,
the one ten years older than me, who
for the first time was away from home.

My mother cared a lot about her husband,
her children, not much about herself.
She was intelligent and beautiful,
enjoyed laughs and smiles.
She was generous, sweet and loving
from her heart, still strict to us.

When she was young,
she was an excellent horseback rider.
At those times she looked happy and free.
After she married, she slowly changed.

She did not talk much about herself.
But there were little hints here and there.
I heard her crying sometimes,
hidden frustration, suffocation,
pain in body and soul. But no big deal,
she always wanted to be strong and perfect.

She died at forty-five,
still young, but looking too old.
I can read her signs now,
I can understand them.

Do I have a chance to free myself
from these hundreds of layers of messiness
which are spinning around her and me,
and our history. I don't know.

I still have a chance, and I hope,
I can write and speak to you,
who will listen and understand.

OBEDIENCE

My mother was ill
as long as I can remember,
mostly lying in her bed.
When she died in 1951
I was nine years old.

Yet on my first day of school
she brought me to my class,
sat in the back of the room,
the one parent present
because I was too afraid
to be without her.

That was the only time
I remembered her being dressed.
For many months she stayed
in sanatoriums, far away from home,
to be cured of her illnesses.
Thrombosis and cancer. At that time,
after the war, there was not much chance.

She was a loving and caring mother
looking out from her bedside
for me and my four older siblings
whenever she could, but also
managing all of us and our huge estate
with lots of maids and gardeners
and even a governess.

She had five children and
also several miscarriages.
All that happened during a ten year
span, from 1932 to 1942,
one of the most tormented times
in German history.

In my memory, which I cherish,
she was good and sweet, but
according to the rules of those days,
during the Nazi regime, she also
obediently followed their law, so
she became a very fruitful mother.

HANNA

She was ten years older than me.
This morning she died.
No more air.
She could not breathe
lying in her husband's arms.

We were five siblings.
Three were younger.
Two were older.
That was the division.
She was the oldest.
Always the one who knew best.

I did not know much about my parents.
They died when I was young,
much too early.
She, my sister, knew more
but she did not tell me.
She kept things to herself.

That summer, the last one,
we came closer to each other.
Invisible barriers were broken.
She gave me pictures, letters, thoughts.
I saw a different side of her.
I felt her softness, her vulnerability.
We connected deeply, sisters.

Pictures come into my mind.
She protecting me
when I was still very young.
Pushing me in a stroller.
Who protected her?
Always the first, the wisest.
Was she ready to die?

My middle sister, the oldest
one of the younger group,
and close to me, said, phoning
from the other side of the ocean,
"She had a smile on her face
when lying in her coffin,
it even got bigger."

She also said,
"You are with us today."
My daughter and my son
were also at her funeral.
That is a comfort, that is peace.
We are together, a family.
I love you, Hanna.

MY FATHER

He was a great grain merchant
in the northern part of Germany
where the landscape is mostly flat,
cornfields as far as your eyes can see.

He died pretty young,
only in his mid-fifties, a stroke,
ten years after his wife passed away,
She with cancer. I was nine years old.

When visiting us on Sanibel Island,
three years ago, my oldest brother
told me that my father was in the NSDAP,
even a member of the SS.

"*Ein passiver Mitläufer,*"
my brother said, no soldier, no officer.
"He stayed at home during the war,
had to look after the grain business.

He did not wear a uniform daily.
Only once a week when he left the house
for a party meeting. After that
he put his uniform in the closet again."

When the war was over he had to go
to the local police to get denazified -
again my brother's memory.
He came back the same day "cleared."

I went to the *Zentralwehrmachtsbüro*
in Berlin to find out more about him.
After a long search, looking intensively
at the computer, the official said:

"Not one entry found, if I were
you, go in peace, let it go."
I did not let it go then, but
I tried to find out in my own way.

What did I know about him?
He was a generous man,
helped people all around him.
Protected his family.

I remember that we five children
were educated beyond nationality.
We visited early in foreign countries
to find our own way into life beyond Germany.

What do I really know about him?
I will never find out completely,
but I feel, I observe, I see, I ask, I hear,
I listen, and that will never end.

WEEKLY MARKET VISITS

Why did it take so many years,
almost to the end of my life,
to recognize that it was you who
gave me moments of safety?

Why did I have to wait so
many hopeless and helpless hours
to find those precious moments
to bring you back to me?

Why did I struggle day after day
to understand what was happening
in my life, but only felt chaos and
confusion inside and outside of me?

The memory of a twelve year old girl,
accompanying her father to the weekly market,
buying fresh cod on Fridays from the friendly
fish lady, me, standing next to you, feeling safe.

The memory of a twelve year old girl,
enjoying my father at the weekly market visit,
getting dark red cherries, eating those delicious
fruits, spitting out the pits on the way home.

Not too long after those market visits you died.
I lost you as I had lost my mother years before,
but these rare moments of feeling safe in our
togetherness will carry me for the rest of my life.

SINS OF THE FATHERS

The sins of the fathers will be felt in the third and
fourth generation. So it is said in *Exodus XX*.
Can I carry that burden, me, one of the countless
second generation Germans of World War II parents?

I carry this heavy load since my birth.
I knew about it as early as I could feel something
without having an idea yet where all this came from.

The burden accompanied me all of my life. I often
pushed it deliberately, forcefully into the background,
but it crawled up to the forefront at its own pleasure and measure.

Books were written by my generation in abundance.
I read many of them, but mostly I could not understand. I felt
that the sins of the fathers often were described as if from
someone else's family. Where was the connection, the real pain?

My children, the third generation, took things more "objectively," but
in their own life many dramas played out, giving me, their mother,
hardly any rest or repose; there was an urge in them to act out
visibly, my acting out was inside, silent.

Today I look at all this chaotic doing not as a wise old woman,
but as someone who only can help and go on if I center myself
into life's love, beauty, forgiveness and joy despite and
because of the close proximity to death and destruction.

Then the sins and burdens of the parents, whatever they were,
can be changed into new possibilities, and the fourth generation
is a blessing. Elena, my granddaughter arrived in time and
my children have again a brighter future, the past less haunting.

FRÄULEIN KLAMA

All five children in our family
had piano lessons with *Fräulein* Klama.
Her fiancé died in World War I, after that
she never had any doubts about being single.
It seemed she liked to be a spinster,
and she loved to be a piano teacher.

After World War II she lived with her mother
in one room of another family's apartment.
Once a week, on Thursdays, she would visit us
in Mielkendorf, staying all day long, enjoying
good food, our spacious house and, most of all,
giving us lessons on a *Steinweg* grand piano.

When he was young, my father had piano lessons
with her as well. She was ancient. But I remember
she was always joyful, never intimidated
by anything, not even after her false teeth stayed
in the dumplings when eating soup with us.
She just put them back in place and smiled.

When my father divorced his second wife, and
my siblings had left home, nobody looked after me.
It was she who cooked a hot meal for me after
school, before our piano lessons started.
It was she who gave me a sense of direction,
since I had none and felt lost.

She played the piano, I would say, with style,
not always hitting each single key precisely,
but she definitely showed the bigger picture.
She brought Mozart and Beethoven, Bach and
Brahms into my life. They kept me going,
sustained me in difficult times and added happy hours.

When she died, I was too busy with myself
and the world and did not go to her funeral.
I regret it deeply. At the end of this poem
for her, I want to thank her for everything
she did for me. She was a very special woman
who brought lots of light to me, her student.

AN ANNOUNCEMENT

The German weekly news magazine *Der Spiegel*
published an article by Dummer early in 2009.
She reported that a study has been conducted
about people born during the time of World War II
(that is sixty-four to seventy years ago)
who have suffered all their lives many different
ailments, including depression, sleeplessness,
dysfunction, sadness, hopelessness and other stuff,
and, as she continues, the children too were part of the deal.

I tried to put these facts into words for a long time. I did
not need a scientific study, but simply observations
of myself, my family and friends, their friends and children
and the environment on both sides of the ocean.
Doing it led me to a similar conclusion by just
feeling out those things. Since the facts are scientifically
acknowledged now, they can be accepted by the world.
Good for those who knew and felt something
long before. We are all safe again.

YOUNG

GUT CHRISTINENTHAL

Gut Christinenthal once had been
the site of the summer residence
of the Danish countess Christina,
close relative to King Christian IV
of Denmark. Her huge estate was
hidden somewhere in Schleswig-Holstein
between the Baltic and North Seas.
She lived in the 18th century and
chose this special spot for herself.
Gut Christinenthal, a place for pleasure.

History indicates that the ownership
of this land between
the two seas was often switched.
Germany, a country of many
little states, owned it from 1871,
the start to the building of a nation state.
When I was born in 1942, in the middle of
World War II, the place belonged
again to Germany, more precisely,
to Hitler's *Deutschen Reich*.
Gut Christinenthal, a place with history.

My grandfather bought this marvel
of seclusion between the First and Second
World Wars. He had become wealthy helping
to build a water connection between the
North and Baltic Seas, *den Nord-Ostsee Kanal*.
The estate turned out to be a wedding present
to my mother, to my parents. Old photos
show her and my father on the occasion of their
engagement. Both enthusiastic horseback riders,
two young, beautiful people in love. They
were beaming while going out for a ride.
My mother's face especially was glowing.
Gut Christinenthal, a place for love.

When World War II was raging,
my whole family and many friends were hiding
in the countless *Gut* buildings to escape
the worst disaster Germany had inflicted
on the world and on itself. I was the only
child born there. Until I was five or six,
we all lived on the estate, crowded together;
the grownups, me and my four older siblings
and lots of other children, somehow connected to us.
We enjoyed every bit of this place,
not knowing the desperate situation
Germany had gotten itself into.
Gut Christinenthal, a sanctuary for children.

How often was I standing in front of the *Gobelins*
covering entire walls of the great dining hall,
following with my eyes the stories of hunters
chasing wild beasts relentlessly.
I, not knowing, that in the world outside
the hunters were chasing Jews, gypsies,
communists and gays and other people.
The outside world for me was in the form
of a huge swing hanging from an umbrella like
red oak tree at the end of our magnificent park,
pumping myself up into the sky as high as I could,
then falling back in pure delight, simply feeling joy.
Gut Christinenthal, a place of innocence.

I visited my place of birth
two or three times later in life.
Each time it had changed owners but
still stayed the same, the beautiful peaceful
hidden spot somewhere between the North
and the Baltic Seas, historically part of
Germany, part of Denmark. Maybe,
so I told myself, it is a place where history
played its tricks on the inhabitants
who belonged to both countries
at different times. It helped me
to understand that roots can grow in
and belong to other places in other times.
Gut Christinenthal, a special place in history.

MIELKENDORF

Several years after the war my parents sold
the huge estate they had received as a wedding gift
from my mother's parents, somewhere
in the middle of Schleswig-Holstein,
where Germans were Danes
and Danes were Germans in history.
The family moved to a different place
near Kiel, a seaport town at the Baltic Sea,
to be closer to my father's grain business.

The location of our new home had no real name
at all. The village Mielkendorf was
two miles away. Our new house,
an old farmstead, was rapidly converted
into ten rooms, receiving constant
enlargements so that the whole family, parents,
five children, gardener, governess and maids
could live in it comfortably.

The small river Eider which crossed through
this northern German state from east to west,
finally finding its way into the North Sea,
meandered between lovely green meadows
very near to our house. A pleasant spot to grow up.
We enjoyed the certain freedom and space
of this landscape, but we did not like the distance
from the city of Kiel, where the real life
for growing up took place. We felt isolated.

Contrary to the scenery, our property was fenced
in with high barbed wire and tall stone walls.
We were separated from the few houses and people
around our estate, yet, inside, we children had
everything we could possibly want.
The many rooms of the house were all occupied
by the family and the people who lived with us.

A huge garden belonged to the new, old estate,
where two to three soccer fields easily could be built.
A German Shepherd on a leash fixed to a steel line
ran up and down his terrain, scaring us
each time we passed his territory.

Another dog was used by my father for hunting.
We saw this dog rarely because he stayed
with the man my father had hired to look after
his hunting property away from our home.
This man also accompanied my father on his trips
into the Austrian Alps to shoot deer with enormous antlers.
My father's young, third wife accompanied him.
She had a child, we had another sibling,
a sweet girl, who I came to love dearly.
She was almost twenty years younger than me.

The antlers of the deer were all fixed onto
wooden boards, the date of the event engraved
on a metal plate, put on each board,
and installed in orderly rows on the walls
of a spacious two car garage. Swallows nested
in the corners of the garage, using the antlers as
springboards to fly out into freedom
through a little window which was left open
for them. The young ones, who had

their first flying lessons in that place,
regularly made our two cars pretty dirty.

We children used the garage, when not occupied,
as our roller skate terrain. Owning just two really
properly working skates, we took turns, or wore only one,
finding our balance by lifting the other foot off the ground.
On the right back side of the garage there were wooden
cabinets with lots of openings for air to pass through.
In fall they got filled with apples from our huge orchard,
tempting us to take one whenever we felt hungry.

My father would come home for lunch
at one, having picked up those of us
who went to girl or boy schools in the city.
Since there was enough help,
a warm meal was ready right on time.
It was served in the dining room
with all members of the household present.
Before eating each of us took
his or her neighbor's hand and in
chorus we said: *Guten Appetit*. Then
my father began to give out the food.

We also had a pig stall with at least twenty
animals, imitating my mother's former estate.
At the peak of the *Gut's* replication
There were even two cows in Mielkendorf.
We sent the milk to be pasteurized and
butter came back with it, later yoghurt too.
Also, we had over a hundred
chickens, laying eggs in special booths which
we children had to watch and keep clean.
Little new chickens came in spring. We never had
any shortage of food after the war.

My second mother sold the eggs from the hens
to the rich ladies she knew in the city who
also became her friends. Once a week,
she drove to town to visit, have tea and
play Bridge with them. This endeavor
took a long time. We loved her being away.
The money earned from the eggs was used
as a vacation fund which we spent each year
on an island at the North Sea. I loved
those times close to the sea more than anything.

My first mother had cancer a long time before
she died. As far as I can remember, she was
always lying in bed in Mielkendorf, unless she
was at a sanatorium in the Black Forest.
When at home, she gave orders and managed
the house from her bedside, so that life would,
despite her severe illness, still run smoothly.
When I visited her in her room, she often gave me
a piece of chocolate mint whose taste
I will never forget. Sometimes she sprayed me
with her perfume, *4711*, a special smell for life.

She knitted sweaters for all the children. My sister
usually got something in red, me in blue.
I never doubted the choice of the colors she made.
I did not doubt so many things when I was young.
I loved her for her gentleness despite her strict authority.
Also, the authority of my father stood
above all our sayings and doings. There was
complete silence and acceptance in respect
to certain things, especially subjects of the past,
which would never be broken by us.
I lived with that silence full of secrets for decades.

Mielkendorf was the place where I spent my youth
from six to fifteen. It all began with
a house full of people, young and old, but when I finally
went to a boarding school in southern Germany,
it was only my father, me and a maid who were left.
My father and his second wife lived separately and
then divorced. He remarried and moved into a new house.
It was my decision to go to school far from
home. My two brothers had been there before.
When I left Mielkendorf, my older siblings
were scattered all over the world, in
Germany, England, Canada and Australia.

By then my mother had been dead for several
years and my second mother had moved back
to the South, where she originally came from.
The two maids eventually married. The gardener,
originally a gifted biologist, got a place at a university.
Her cousin, our governess, found a job as a
public school teacher, and we children saw each other
rarely during these years. My father died in 1961.
Everything fell into or out of place.
There was no longer a center where we could go.

Many years passed and personal things
happened to each of us.
My oldest sister died. The structure changed.
We remaining siblings became
closer again, all of us living in different countries.
Many more years passed and personal things
happened to each of us. At the end
my youngest brother took his life. The structure changed again.
We, who remain, talk on the phone and try to see
each other somewhere in the world.
I had to find out more about the silence
which webbed around parents and children.
I feel it is my duty. I will do it all by myself.

UNDER THE TULIP TREE

How old was I
when I was lying under the little tulip tree
in our huge garden,
looking through the leaves into the blue sky?
Not one dark cloud.

How happy was I
when I touched
the pink and white soft flower petals
caressing me back without resistance.
Not one sad feeling.

How innocent was I
when I smelled the fresh cut green grass;
my young soft body naked,
greeting each blade with pleasure.
Not one joyless spot.

How young was I
when I tasted the red, thick strawberries
growing in abundance year after year
close to the beautiful tulip tree.
Not one bad fruit.

I was a little girl,
not older than six or seven,
dreaming about my mother,
ill and often away from home.
Hardly any day together.

I, wishing and praying that
she would come back,
healthy and strong,
lying close to me under the tulip tree
in our huge garden.

SÜDFRIEDHOF

To reach my high school
I had to bicycle almost
an hour from our home
in the countryside to the city.

First I rode along green meadows
with grazing cows, sometimes horses,
a few farms at the side of the road, then
came the suburbs with single family houses.

The last part of my ride took me into
the beginning of the city. I had to pass
an endlessly long street with a red brick wall.
Hidden behind it was a huge cemetery, the *Südfriedhof*.

Having conquered that distance, my school
showed up, the Käthe Kollwitz *Schule*.
When classes were done, I often rode
to the cemetery, passed through an iron gate and

walked into my sacred space. Stillness started.
Old oak trees, thick bushes, stone walls and
nicely cut hedges surrounded the graves, decorated
with pretty flowers in spring and summer.

To me all this felt like a maze. Still, I knew my way,
first for awhile straight ahead, the wide main path
till I came to a big chestnut tree, then bear left,
a wooden cross showed up, a minister's grave.

A short walk again to the left, finally a sharp right turn
and I had reached my destination, my mother's grave.
I often collapsed at the end of the plot and started
to cry, she, having left me forever some time ago.

This was the place to be closest to her. I felt
lonely, without any protection, open to all kinds
of vulnerability, I also felt ugly, not very worthy
of anything, a beginning teenager, just growing up.

I, lying now on the grave, touching the soil,
felt the need to come here to get food
for my hungry soul, so that I could go on with life and
connect with her who was physically disconnected.

Riding my bicycle home, I was eager to reach
the green meadows, crossing the little creek,
wild dandelions all over the place. They
gave me joy and a feeling of belonging again.

IN FRONT OF THE TATE

It was a warm summer day.
They both were sitting on a long old wooden bench
in front of the Tate Gallery in London, overlooking
the Thames, each in one corner.
He, the professor of linguistics from Connecticut,
USA, on his way to a conference in Salzburg.
She, a teacher of English from Hamburg, Germany,
on her way to her sister's vacation place in Wales.

A conversation started carefully. It slowly led to going
into the Tate and looking at the breathtaking Turners,
the reason both had come to this place first of all.
Turner, the modern painter of the 19th Century, who often
let the objects swim and disappear in a sea of color
only guessing where the subjects could have been hidden.

They stayed and enjoyed the London cultural scene,
the daily life, the British Museum, a play called *Wild Oats*
at the Strand, Covent Garden with quiche and red wine.
Later they drove to Salisbury, visited the magnificent cathedral
(she loved to visit churches), ending up in Bath with
 Roman remnants where they said farewell for good.

Somehow the professor figured out her address in Hamburg, though
she had not given it to him. They wrote a few letters back and forth,
but the situation was not good, and they soon stopped writing.
Three years later she got a phone call from London,
the connection was terrible, the phone numbers were not right
and again further plans did not materialize.

One more year passed and a postcard arrived from Salzburg at her house. The professor had a sabbatical. They met in Münster, Westphalia, one week later. It was a neutral place. After that they stayed together till today. There seemed to be no other plan for them. Jewish German history with a new old connection began a long journey into unchartered territory. Love and their children were the only things they could offer.

THE ATLANTIC CROSSING

It took us almost two weeks
to cross the Atlantic.
This was some decades ago.
Now we fly from Boston to London
in six hours,
eating chicken teriyaki or pink salmon.
The way back home takes one hour longer.
The jet stream plays a role.
Six hours, seven hours, two weeks.
How long did it take Columbus?
Does it matter?
There is always this beautiful blue ocean
when the sun is shining,
and the grey black roaring sea in heavy storms.
It separates the people here and there,
not only through its mysterious waters
but through the unspoken gestures and words,
swimming in the deep of the sea
or dancing on top of the waves,
understanding its meaning differently at both shores.
Although time and space are connected,
still somehow they have their own different lives.
But if I stand on the beach at Cape Cod,
I touch the same water as people in Brighton or Bremen.
Then I feel there is a bridge over the blue and black ocean
which nobody can destroy.

MY COUNTRY

Where can I go in a country
that is not my own?
Where can I be
in a place full of strangers,
where families are happy together,
although they don't know
what to be happy for?
Where children are challenged
to be something other than themselves?
Where even dogs get food
for happiness on TV?
Let me tell you,
this country is exhausting
despite its magnificence and beauty.
Let me tell you,
I question this country,
and love it at the same time.
It is a country full of mystery.
It is my country.

OLIVER

He was a smart, little boy
who you had to like and love.
When he started the *Gymnasium*
he got a light brown leather bag.
It was the fashion at that time.
Every morning he raced to school
on his bike, arriving just in time
to take his seat,
still out of breath.

He came with me to the U.S.
when he was a teenager.
After one year
he went back to Germany
to live his own life
and to finish the *Abitur*.
Coming again to America,
he followed his passion,
learning and doing film.
NYU in New York
was the place to be.
His first movie was called
Magda, an amazing story.
Proudly he dedicated it to us.

Back to Germany, to Hamburg,
then Berlin, getting married,
a place to rest.
His eyes always seeing things
others did not.
Where will he go next?
He needs lots of love and stability,
as we all do.
But still,
he can live here and there
because his mind is open
and his heart is soft and big.
We might see more from him
in the future,
nurturing our imagination,
the smart, little boy in him.

VANESSA

She was wearing
a red and white sweater
and a red skirt
the first day of school.
She looked so sweet and joyful
among all the children,
carrying a huge backpack
on her small shoulders.

She is older now,
a real woman,
beautiful and intelligent.
Looking with her grey blue eyes
through you,
as if telling you
that she understands
the sorrow and the pain
a girl has experienced,
who was courageous enough
to be too much herself,
full of demands and joy.

She was hurt deeply,
and destruction came with it.
Now she is wiser.
Her speech has slowed down.
She talks with more knowledge
and less spontaneity.
Limits have been set forcefully.
History can't be surpassed easily.

But she still has this sudden,
happy laughter, coming from
deep within, unexpectedly.
Then I know that her world
goes on and even if
heavy storms strike,
she does not let go.
Golden rays always carry her.

DAISY

It was early in the morning,
a white winter day.
Snow had fallen over night.
She came into this world
with Beethoven and Mozart
in a friendly hospital room,
David standing next to me.
She was a precious flower
from the beginning on,
and I, at that biblical age,
proud to have such a sweet baby.
Now she is almost as tall as I am.
We start to talk more like women
although the little girl still
hides behind each sentence.

What will the future bring to her?
Can I understand her deepest desires,
sense her hidden hopes and
see what gives her strength? Or
will the world go on faster and faster,
giving her less and less time
to sit down and just
look at the beautiful nature around her,
so that she will not fall apart
when the world spins off?
I am sure she won't forget
the trees or the flowers
or the faces around her,
in pain, joy and love. I know her.
She is a Daisy.

PAIN

PATTERNS THAT CONNECT

It is wonderful
to talk about patterns
that connect.
Bateson looked deep into it.
Fascinating.
We all want to connect
because we are connections.

What if the patterns that connect
are not the ones that connect
in a good way?
What if they are the reason
for destruction and desolation?

We have to learn to see those patterns
and to break them.
It means looking inside
more than we are used to.
Turning upside down
the dispositions and predispositions
we are familiar with.

Opening our hearts and
listening not only to the words
but the words behind the words.
Lots of movement and commotion,
inside out and outside in.

The answer will come,
sometimes slowly
if I connect with you, you with me.
The painful breaking moves over
into joyful reconnecting.

We are ready to start again
with patterns that connect.
The future is now.

DESPAIR FOR THE WORLD

When despair for the world grows in me,
I leave the self behind
and all the things
which seem insurmountable at this moment.
I put them in a box
and throw them over my shoulder.
They vanish through space and time
into the universe.

When despair for the world grows in me,
I leave behind the millions of crooked patterns of thought
which fly around in my head relentlessly,
I catch them in a deep mood of urgency
and let them escape into the universe,
through space and time again
over my shoulder.

Having done these necessary tasks,
I go into the garden,
twist and twirl around
till I fall into the green grass,
my eyes take in the wide, blue, heavenly sky,
my body feels the cool, soothing mother earth.

I stretch out my arms and
pick with two fingers
a tiny little daisy,
sweet, white and yellow.
My heart feels connected and whole.
Unconditional love.
Then I may say
I rest in the grace of the world, and I am free.

MAY FLOWERS

Why do I write down words
if I know that they can't say
what I want to say?
Why do I write them down
despite the fact that they are
not born here?

They don't have the easiness
belonging to the owner.
My words are simple ones,
not from a mouth
trained for centuries
in verse and rhyme
in the English language.
Still, I feel good
writing them down
because they don't carry the history
of my mother tongue.

They don't carry the load of a nation
which brought into life
existential thoughts and subtle poetry
as well as beautiful music,
but also the cruelest war
in history.

Here I am naked
despite haunting memories
that live with me.
I try to bring things out differently
by starting fresh again,
like May flowers,
which just open their buds,
shy and innocent, yet
nothing can stop them.

So I write down my words
in this beautiful language,
knowing that the truth will
reveal itself eventually.

JONAH'S *YOM KIPPUR*

Jonah was fast asleep
in the middle of a huge storm.
The sailors on the boat
tried to keep their precious vessel in balance.
But they unbalanced it by throwing out all the ballast.

God had asked Jonah to go and help Nineveh.
Nineveh was in trouble.
Jonah preferred to be fast asleep
while the sailors worked for him.
He was in trouble too.

Nineveh was not his country, not his language.
Why go there?
Jonah just did the opposite.
Why is it so easy to run away
instead of doing what You say?

Jonah went deeper down.
He stayed in a huge whale.
He preferred to be dead
better than being alive
and doing the right thing.

Why do we hear You and don't listen?
We are afraid of everything,
You included.
You give us a new start.
That is more than we can ever ask for.

Jonah was saved.
Yom Kippur is for all of us.

MY HEART

My heart is heavy,
heavy from the load
I carry around for centuries.
My heart is full of suffocation.
Is there no one
who can lift the heavy load?
Is there nobody
who can understand
that being alive means being alive and dead
at the same time?

Where is the happiness of easy living
I sometimes experienced
when feeling young at heart?
I get a glimpse of it here and there.
These days I am longing for it,
like a little girl
who knows the pleasure
of doing something right.

Now where my body is frail,
I feel I have the right to know
how to lift the heavy load,
if only a bit now and then.
Don't give up on me
since only you know my heart.

BURNT OUT

It did not start today, yesterday,
or the day before.
It started long ago.
Little signs here and there.
Then the cough began,
feelings of exhaustion,
but somehow I could not believe it.
I was a smart, intelligent woman.
Two successful grown up children
on the other side of the Atlantic,
a third child at forty-five.
A doctorate several years later,
tackling science, philosophy and religion,
the whole world on paper.

A second marriage of love, also differences
contradictions and ambiguities.
My body and soul cried for help,
relentlessly.
I did not even know
how to face them.
Caring, working, being everywhere,
nobody can do that
for such a long time,
contemplating everything.
Now I start to listen, to listen carefully,
to all the voices of my mind, body and soul.
They like me, and slowly I like them.
It is a simple as that.
No hidden secrets.

WINTER IN NEW ENGLAND

Each winter in New England
brings me closer to Emily Dickinson.
Around the middle of January
when it is really getting cold,
there starts this deep desire in me
to stay in our cozy Cape Cod like house,
to be just inside and to enjoy the pleasures
which this seclusion brings to me.

In former times when I knew
so much less about myself,
I would get sick, helplessly
and seriously, but now,
when the heavy snow, the gusty winds,
icy rain or even crispy sunshine starts,
I know that the time has come again
to begin the journey inside and within.
What was pain and despair before,
now gets mixed with pleasure and delight.

These winter days which I mostly experience
through the little window panes
everywhere in our white wooden home,
guide me on the road to my happy heart
and to the many others that are dear to me,
by just being still, drinking in the silence,
the richness of this soothing winter time.
I open my eyes to the whiteness of the snow
and embrace the world in a way,
yes, maybe, just as Emily Dickinson did.

DISTORTED VIEW

When the sun is shining outside,
and the snow does not feel so cold anymore,
I get a feeling of spring even if
it is only the middle of March.
Then it hits me especially hard
to be the only person in the family
burdened by a distorted view, the only one
who looks at things differently from the others.
At those moments I try to breathe deeply,
to relax, take a warm bath and think positively.
Yet all these tricks don't help at those
crucial times. They show even more
how vulnerable I am and how little
understanding there seems to be of me.

When it comes to the basics I know that
I don't really belong to them. I feel
that my talking and gestures are seen
as not fitting. I and my children laugh
at different moments. I can't shout hurrah
when they give endless compliments
to each other to show how wonderful
they are. I just gasp for air to get
over the next coup. I feel I am lost
in a black hole and will never
come out again.

Suddenly I look inside myself.
Wasn't there the little, cheerful girl
who could laugh unpretentiously
over some silly, innocent jokes?
Wasn't there the cheerful, little girl
who would jump into the snow,
lying on her back now, creating
a perfect angel using her hands
and feet in regular motions?
I know she is there, much older
but still alive and well.
Why all this agonizing and hiding?
Why this distorted view? Who can judge?
Just be who you are, then
everything will fall into place.

RED APPLES IN WHITE SNOW

Red apples in white snow,
beautiful, lonely, cheerful.
I cherish the whole wonder.
Breathing deeply in and out
the air I still can catch.

My lungs don't allow the full measure.
To be content with less is enough.
Less is more than I thought of.
Less is healing, walking, writing.
Less is me, my family and friends,
and coming closer to nature again.

I still take in enough air to embrace
the wonders of the world,
breathing deeply,
inside out, outside in.
Yes, red apples in white snow
bring gratitude, beauty and joy.

A DAHLIA

My breasts cry.
My lungs suffer.
My heart weeps.

One red dahlia
was brought
to my house
by a friend
whose breasts
also cried -
a long time ago.

Now this one
dark red
star-like dahlia
gives so much
love and light
to me.

JOY

THE FARM

When I walk on the farm
I talk to the flowers and the grass.
The clouds send greetings with their many shapes.
The trees wave their crowns against the blue sky,
assuring me that it is good to be here and
to breathe the fresh air which blows over the green meadows.
All worries fly away when taking step after step.
I slowly climb up the hill and finally reach the top,
proud that my lungs did not burst.
Then my eyes wander into the far distance,
jumping over the tops of beautiful carpets of trees.
I play with this magnificent view
like a child at the ocean.
I am standing still, and I feel
life as an infinite circle of ebb and flow,
of living and dying and living again.
Here I am, happy to be a part of this earth.

FROM HEAVEN TO EARTH AND UP AGAIN

Up the hill on the farm
a huge meadow stretches
in front of me.
On this sunny day
fresh green grass
is speckled with
hundreds of dandelions.
I pick one up.
Hundeblume - dog flower,
we say in German.
It sounds so demeaning.
Dandelion has more melody.

The dandelions look content,
sheltered by the juicy grass.
Their blossoms bow this way
and that, greeting each other
with happy anticipation.

My eyes take in this pastoral scene.
They absorb every bit of it,
and carry it into my body and soul.
Joyfulness spreads through me.
My eyes wander from the meadow up
to the sky, one flowing into the other,
there is no breaking point,
and everything looks sacred.

All my grumbles and complaints,
negativity and neglect,
get washed away. They fly out as if
body and soul don't want any
inside-outside-inside drama anymore.
They want to stick to something sweeter.
Bitterness doesn't taste good.
They want to immerse fully
in the dandelion-grass-sky womb,
as if in a bubbling bubble bath,
completely covered by gratitude.
With one dandelion in my hand,
I am open now to anything
from heaven to earth and up again.

WALKING AT THE FENTON RIVER

The Fenton River is not far from our home,
a short steep path through the woods
down to the Grist Mill and we are there.

On this sunny, almost hot, early spring day
the river shows itself from its finest side
as we walk on a narrow trail just beside it.

The softly moving water talks to us
in a peaceful way, bubbling on and on;
it never questions, it never stops.

We halt to understand its secret messages,
yet we only see how crystal clear it is now,
showing us precious gems of glittering stones.

Several tall trees have fallen across the river:
a natural bridge,
a testimony to former, rougher times.

Today, little tender trout-lilies and fragile trillium
peak out of the soil, next to the moving water,
greeting us with their yellow and red blossoms.

First signs of spring. We happily enjoy the walk,
especially the stretch through the pine woods.
Golden rays of sun are falling into it, dreamlike.

Taking step after step on this beautiful day,
our friend shows us the direction. No confusion.
We follow it confidently, on the path back as well.

Thus finding our way, something incredible happens.
We slowly feel as if the river, the flowers, the woods
expand to one unity; everything becomes one.

We all belong together, nature, woman, man.
Nothing can separate us now. Even hours and days
after the walk a feeling of wholeness is still with us.

RED HIBISCUS

Your open blossom
with soft petals
leads me into a sea of love
and sweet tenderness.

Your stem guides me
to a beautiful heart,
takes off my sadness and
fills me with hope and joy.

MY HEART AGAIN

My heart is light, light with the joy
I carry around for some time now.
My heart is full of love,
since there is always somebody
who understands
that being alive means
giving and receiving,
asking and forgiving
at the same time.

Where is the sadness of living
so often experienced
when feeling old at heart.
It has not gone.
I still know this feeling
from being a little girl
who wanted the pleasure
of doing something right.

Now when my body is frail
but alive again,
I feel I have the duty to tell
how to lift a heavy load
and turn it into lightness
each day a bit more.
Just ask, don't give up.
Serve and obey
and reach for happiness.

WAKING UP

I don't open my eyes yet.
Let them be still closed
in this state of nowhereness.
Let them be on their own,
not yet touching the many objects
which will jump up
as soon as my eyelids move
from down to up.
I love this state of floating.

Am I dreaming, am I not?
I really can't tell.
There is this lightness of being.
Yet at the same time I feel
the heaviness of my body,
sense each bone through my flesh
touching the soft surface underneath,
giving the message:
I am alive, I am well.

My mind still wanders
back to where I came from
in this special sleeping/waking state.
It crosses borders, touches the sky,
rides on the clouds,
brings me to places instantly,
here and across the ocean.
No time zones, no language barriers.
Words understood, gestures welcomed
perfectly translated.
Laughter and joy are combined.

There is a freshness in the air.
Enthusiasm all over and
the wind takes everything
I can think of at this moment
of sleeping and waking
and I know, if I open my eyes now,
some of all this lightness will remain,
and it will carry through
to you and me.

A SIMPLE WOMAN

It is as if the clouds of darkness
hanging over me for sixty years,
have finally gone out of the center of my being.
The dragging, unexplainable weight,
always as heavy as wet snow,
melted away over the last years.

I can't say this came suddenly.
It was a long journey
of opening up old scars and wounds
sitting in my soul and body,
not willing to move one little bit.

Yet there were these many friends,
inside and outside of me,
who did not stop, who did not give up
poking me into each single corner,
to find new ways to wake me up,

to show me that life has more to offer
than wet snow, dark clouds and blocked views.
Each one of them asked and provoked me
to be honest, to confront myself
with myself, so that at the end

there was this me, stripped of the mess,
the dirt, the creepiness, to reach the other side,
the authentic me; not striving to be
more than she can carry,
a *simple* woman with joy for the earth,
the water, the wind, the sky and the sun.

She says now yes to a complicated, complex world
by letting go of all false pretense,
by letting in love and peace and
accepting without shame
a divine power
which guides us all.

THE OCEAN

The ocean carries me in a way
no one else ever did before,
by never really being still,
always on the go, on top
the waves with their white crowns,
deep down a mass of moving water
pushing itself in all different directions.
Still as a whole it has the tenacity
and strength of a never bursting bubble,
safe.

The ocean waits for someone like me
to be carried candidly, and by doing so
it provokes stories, evokes memories
which were sleeping for years or decades
hidden somewhere in my body and mind.
Nobody now in between.
The connection is perfect.
The conversation can begin.

ELENA

Waves when looking out of the window,
curling crests dancing on top.
Together they move steadily to the shore,
the beach halts them,
rolling out as a whirling white.
They arrive at their destination
and give me the message
of the deep connection
to my grandchild,
even if so far away.

She, still a baby,
will feel our bond,
as I do, even more than words
and gestures can say.
She, not one year old
and not yet using words intelligently,
will feel that there is a language
beyond all talking
which does not need interpretation.

THE QUESTION OF HOME

Elena, my little granddaughter, comes for a visit
to our winter place in Florida, far from her home
in Germany, where I lived for forty years.
Home is a concept now nestled and
hidden in my heart. I can feel it
at certain times and places.
It is good as it is.

Elena, I think, will stay where she is.
Her mother, my daughter, as a teenager
once lived together with us in the U.S.,
having left her childhood home behind.
She knows about those things. She persists
in being in a place where you long belong to
and that is good as well.

You, my mother, the unknown grandmother
of my children, knows about it. You had a grave
with a gravestone in the *Südfriedhof* in Kiel.
I always needed to see you there to get strength.
My father, your husband, lay next to you.
One day your grave was brutally destroyed.
It was not good.

Now you have a new place, a round fieldstone
on top of the hill on the university farm
in Connecticut. You have got a view into
the far distance, even to the other side of
the big ocean, to your old home in Germany.
You can see all of us, and we can see you.
Finally, everything is good again.

GRACE

OPEN THE EYES OF MY EYES

Open the eyes of my eyes.
Please open them now.
They are the ones who see
what I can't see.
They are the ones who
open up the world
I really want to be in.
Each single day is a journey
to find the path to wholeness.
It is a path which offers joy,
happiness and simple abundance
by accepting suffering and pain
at the same time.
It is a path which brings me
into the richness of my being
and looks at all other people
near and far with new eyes.
Even evil gets turned around
into something I can face,
and joy becomes contagious.
I-Thou is real. It goes both ways.
The eyes of my eyes become one.

THE BARBERSHOP ON HENRY STREET

David's father had a barbershop
on Henry Street in New York
on the lower east side of Manhattan.
After coming from Drohitchen,
a little village in Russia,
in the middle of the 1920s,
he gave up resting on Sabbath.
The barbershop was the source of life
for him and his family.
So he needed this day.
The rabbi, who often walked by the window
of the shop, showed
that he did not approve.
Yet for David's father the work was existential
and an expression of his newly gained freedom.
It was his way of leaving behind
the shtetl in Russia for a new shtetl,
the barbershop, a center of communication,
a place to be.

When David became head
of his department
at the university,
he created his own shop.
Teachers were a unit of consensus,
they did good and interesting work.
Students related to them
as if they were their equals.
Professors and students cared for
and looked after each other.
All events, from Ph.D.s to births
were celebrated in a welcoming way.
For David, the department was a further step
to freedom, a new shop, a new shtetl,
a place to be.

When David retired, after many years
of putting his heart into his work,
there was still enough time to reflect on
and to tackle the rest of his life.
David started to play the piano again,
he approached the playing methodically,
he wanted to know the theory
behind the black and white notes.
He felt comfortable in his home.
From time to time he went back
to his old department/shop
where he fit right in.
But he also found freedom
in his new way of living.
He even went to a discussion group
led by an insightful rabbi,
to dig deep into biblical texts,
professionally of course.
His shtetl expanded more and more
and became filled with life and soul
which father and son had created
over many years.
A home to be.

ABUNDANCE

If I am in myself
I am happy about almost everything.
The grass, the trees, the flowers,
the house I live in,
the rooms, the carpets, the chairs and tables,
the piano, so often in use,
the kitchen, the pots and pans,
the food we eat, bread and also wine.
I think how rich I am.
I think of the family and friends around me,
especially, David with passion at the piano,
and walking Tuffy, our dog,
cooking and looking
after neatness in the kitchen.

Daisy, jumping on the trampoline,
doing her homework,
talking endlessly with friends
never forgetting Tuffy.
Oliver, the film maker, in Berlin,
experiencing daily the clash
between east and west.
Vanessa, in Hamburg,
becoming a journalist,
investigating art and culture
on both sides of the Atlantic.

Rebekah, with Eric, in Boston.
loving Thai Chi, and her dog Loki.
Susannah, in Madison, Wisconsin,
enjoying languages, Hebrew as well,
knowing the secrets of traditional recipes.
Bubbi, in New York, always
giving the latest news on the phone
and preparing kosher food for us.

My parents, long gone, but
coming closer to me every day.
And me, between pots and pans,
Gershwin, Mozart and Mendelssohn,
have this feeling of simple abundance
when I am in myself, and
today with family and friends around
at Daisy's Bat Mitzvah.

A LATE SUMMER MORNING

When I stepped out on the porch
my heart almost stopped.
The beauty of this late summer morning.
The air so clear.
The sun brilliantly brightened the backyard.
Tall trees, surrounding our property,
looked majestic in their green dresses.
Only here and there yellow or red leaves
showed up shyly, still in waiting.

I sat down at the breakfast table
with David, in the shade of the porch.
Daisy, happy to come and go.
With each bite of bread
I took in the moments
of this precious late summer morning,
storing them in my body,
to keep them safe for the coming winter.

Wasn't it here just one month ago,
the celebration of Daisy's Bat Mitzvah,
where the backyard had become a sacred place
for family and friends, gathering together
to listen to what secrets exist
between God and us,
told through Daisy's reading
of the story of Ruth,
her celebration of friendship.
The rabbi's carefully led discussion,
and poems and words from all of us,
the singing, praying and praising,
and finally the joy of belonging.

Everything was connected,
past, present and future,
family and friends, through
nature and mind.
What happened then was a miracle.
I know this now,
with each bite of bread,
this beautiful late summer morning
on the porch in our backyard.

A BORROWED NIGHT

I dreamed last night that after
fifty-five years of silence
my mother was back.

I felt the utmost joy
that she was here
with me. Before,

I never allowed myself
to make room for her,
inside and outside.

It was too painful.
She had left me
too young and too soon.

Now we came together again,
completely natural,
giving love and being loved.

It was a borrowed night.
I knew
she would go again.

Yet in this precious dream
we made up for all the time
separate and alone.

THE COUPLE

Walking along the wide empty beach in the evening
on Hutchinson Island. It is not really warm in early March,
quite windy. They wear their rain gear for protection.
Waves with white crowns are rolling onto the sand,
the sky full of clouds, reddish, purple and blue colors.

They, the couple, married for quite a long time,
for both of them second marriages.
Having gone through life's incredible challenges,
leaving behind old wounds and scars.

She, coming from the other side of the ocean,
having two great grown up children living there,
even a sweet grandchild. All loved dearly.

He, an American, born Jewish, still
feeling a different history, tradition
and sense of belonging.

She, a German, born in the middle
of World War II, history of another kind
burdening her, tragedy in her bones.

His father and mother from the Russian-Polish
border, his mother's parents and little sister
killed in a concentration camp. Speaking of tragedy.

He, a linguist, professor emeritus,
lots of career and knowledge, knowing
now that this alone does not count.

She, Ph.D. completed after their marriage.
She can't deny his claim.
Always looking for something subtler.

He, having two good grown up girls
from his previous marriage. They,
both knowing a lot about life.

The couple is happy to have had
one child together, late for them both.
She, amazingly tender, connected to all.

They go on walking silently.
It is a serene atmosphere. Nothing now
could be more beautiful, more complete.

They know their secrets, and although
they don't talk, they support each other here
and on their long journey together.

FRIEDRICHSKOOG

A place nobody really knows
somewhere on the map
between Germany and Denmark,
behind the dike at the North Sea,
nowhere land.

A place where I can rest,
where time stands still
and sky and earth meet
wherever I look,
flat land.

A place to feel
present, past and future,
rough and gently combined,
seeing the whole picture,
timeless land.

A place where nature
speaks to me
through wind, storm and sun,
clouds, light and rain,
nature's land.

A place that heals
many hurts and wounds,
and sets me free
to start a new day
with hope, faith and love,
healing land.

THE FAMILY REUNION

AT THE NORTH SEA

We all met in Friedrichskoog
behind the dike, on the dike and
before the dike in the endless *Watt*.

My sister Gitta from England
with her husband, two of their children
and three lively grandchildren.

My brother Hans from Canada with his wife.
My brother Juergen's son and his two lovely
young girls from near Kiel.

Juergen, himself, decided not to come.
His self imposed isolation from family
prefigured his lonely death.

My little sister Connie, her husband
and three nice daughters made the trip
from Southern Germany.

Connie's mother, my father's third wife,
came as well. She took the train from Bad Harzburg,
the first mountain area after the Northern lowlands.

Oliver, with his racing bike, arrived from Berlin,
Vanessa and husband Uli and my sweet
granddaughter Elena, from Hamburg.

Susannah flew in from Madison, Wisconsin,
Daisy, from our home in Connecticut,
and David and I sailed by boat over the ocean.

Jockel, my former husband, Oliver's and
Vanessa's father, with his friend Janet,
embracing the Hamburg-London connection.

My Cousin Kurt, my father's brother's son,
came from Kiel. Also many other relatives
more distantly related, all happy to come.

We were forty people, two full days together.
Beautiful and precious hours with sunshine,
wind and the North Sea always around us.

A first evening in a rustic village barn,
Oliver grilling meat, sausages; lots of eating
and talking to get to know each other again.

Next noon, when the tide was out, we all
walked onto the *Watt*, endlessly brown
mud on our feet and legs. More connecting.

The afternoon with volley ball
for the youth, parents sitting at the side
admiring the players' flexibility and fun. Later

champagne on the dike with a soft breeze
and the sun still out, more connecting,
laughter, surprises and remembering.

A dinner in the *Mövenkieker*, everybody
feeling good, the harmonious atmosphere contagious.
Photos on the tables, the past came up.

What did I think about all this joyfulness,
knowing that we all carry German history
in our bodies and souls and still live with it.

It seemed to me that our parents finally
joined us here to reconcile, to make peace with
us, we with them. We now were close again.

Even though we look at our common history
from quite different perspectives, there was forgiveness,
understanding, acceptance and enjoyment in the air.

For me it was closure after all the countless
years of feeling a victim and feeling guilt,
A coming home, a pass to freedom.

This is how I felt, never forgetting, always remembering,
having open questions, sensing some kind of miracle.
I can always talk to you, and you answer me.

IN CONNECTICUT

We all met in our cozy Cape Cod like house
in Connecticut to celebrate Thanksgiving.
It is the first time again after a long break.

Bubbi came from New York with Carol,
David's sister, and her husband Robert,
loaded with chocolate and cheese cakes.

Molly, Carol's daughter, and Kyle,
her boyfriend, showed up early, bringing
wine, bagels and bialys and Manhattan air.

Rebekah and Susannah, David's daughters,
brought with them a cousin from France,
arriving a day before. A great support crew!

Then there were David, me and Daisy, having
already shopped and made beds so that
everybody could feel comfortable from the start.

There was activity all over the house,
especially in the kitchen, where Rebekah and
David prepared the turkey and the stuffing.

Lots of cutting vegetables and fruit to come up
with delicious warm and cold dishes, of course
yams and cranberries and pumpkins with parsley.

It all took a long time, talking and noshing,
laughing and showing, forgetting and remembering,
setting the table and preparing for closeness.

When we finally gathered in the dining room,
finding our seats and starting to relax,
we realized what a present it was to be here now.

We said thanks for many things, each of us, for
the good food, for our health, for the family, there I
added that we have family on both sides of the ocean.

Jewish past was dominant mixed with French,
Italian and Irish stories. It seemed to me that
we joined here to reconcile, to make peace.

What did I think about all this coziness,
knowing that I carry German history in my
body and soul and Daisy carries both.

For me it was closure after all the countless
years of feeling a victim and feeling guilt,
A coming home, a pass to freedom.

This is how I felt, never forgetting, always remembering,
having open questions, sensing some kind of miracle.
I can always talk to you, and you answer me.

SPACE AND TIME

I need space,
more and more space
to make room, so my inside and outside
world can expand boundlessly.

I need time,
more and more time, so
this newly created universe can
be filled endlessly.

I sense an urgency
to grab the space and fill it out
with thoughts and things, precious ones,
and watch over them carefully and

take the time, experience
each tiny bit of it excessively and
feel how it is to be alive
in this sacred timeless time.

Finally, to say thanks to all
who are part of this journey and
have given me the gift of knowing
and feeling blessed.

THANK YOU

How can I say it right
at the end of my journey.
Thank you, thank you for everything.
There is so much to be thankful for.

I start with the big ocean and the North Sea
(you know by now how much I love water)
David, my kids, his kids and our kid,
Bubbi, my parents and our grandchild Elena,
the entire family and friends here and there.

I thank you for the sun, the moon, the stars,
for the whole universe,
for talking to me and restraining me, for partly
deconstructing and reconstructing me new.

I thank you for taking away what I don't need.
Giving so much, letting go and setting me free,
for living step by step, taken now with more care,
for understanding, accepting, enjoying and having

sent me on this incredible and amazing journey
which is yours as well, where all people and
things do connect at the end in a miraculous way.
Thank you, Gd.

EPILOGUE

FOR MY YOUNGER BROTHER

His death was such an earthshaking act
which had to be grasped somehow and
when it got more bearable for me, for us,

I had to give him the place he deserved.
Without doing that I would have failed
to convey my deepest feelings.

As horrible as my brother's death was,
it revealed with clarity
the path he went along and all alone.

It also revealed what it meant
to be born in World War II.
As a German boy he was burdened

with the silence of our parents and the country.
I can understand him now, his self-imposed
isolation and utter desperation.

He tried to keep up with the demands
of the world around him and with
his own difficult family, missing guidance

how to be himself. Bitterness nestled in him.
He did not know to open up, to talk, to defend,
to forgive himself and others, to be free.

Today I am stunned to say that
 I go on living despite obstacles
and lingering illnesses.

Through his death he challenged me to be
even more aware of life's entanglements
and to embrace them fully.

Let him be with me, with us,
now unconditionally, for
he in spirit is with me and you.

ACKOWLEDGEMENTS

Many people helped this book come to publication. I thank them all dearly. I thank also those who have given gifts beyond literary support. Susanne Davis, who from the moment I showed her my first poems in 2008, did not doubt that I could create this book of poetry. Her courage, enthusiasm and love were sustaining. Aurora Milvae helped put the book into shape.

Joan Sidney Seliger's adult writing workshop "Writing for Your Life" around her dining room table is the place where miracles happen. I joined the group in 1997. Joan has the gift to create an atmosphere of trust and understanding. Alice, Anne, Beth, Jane, Janis, Liz B., and Liz T. are always very encouraging.

The Windham Area Poetry contest selected three of my poems. "My Country" won a first place in 2000, "Red Apples in White Snow" was "Honorable Mention" in 2002. "The Atlantic Crossing" was published in the Long River Magazine of the Connecticut Poetry Society in 2010, "May Flowers" is forthcoming in 2011. In 2000 I published ten poems in the "Gentle Actions Newsletter No 8" from the "Gentle Actions Institute for Holistic Studies" which I had founded in 1996. The Gentle Actions Ladies were inspiring in their thinking and actions. The International Women's Writing Guild (IWWG), with its director Hannelore Hahn, is a wonderful support. Anne Buchalski, my massage therapist, connects gently mind, body and soul. Acupuncturist Deborah Pacik lets my energy flow. Dori is our Dori.

My sister and older brother are always there for me. My children Oliver, Vanessa and Daisy and my stepchildren Rebekah and Susannah, each in their own way contributed to the writing of these poems . They showed me how blessed I am with all of them. Bubbi, my mother-in law, touched me deeply by always being Bubbi. Carol, her daughter, wisely commented on my draft. Finally I introduce my husband David, without whom this whole undertaking would not have been possible. For almost thirty years he has been there for me and helped me to do my best. Words are totally inadequate. There are family members and friends whom I did not mention. I apologize. May they all know how much I appreciate their support.

19355739R00069

Made in the USA
Charleston, SC
19 May 2013